TINY DOGS

PAPILLONS

by Allan Morey

Consultant: Jennifer Zablotny
Doctor of Veterinary Medicine
American Veterinary
Medical Association

Pebble®
Plus

CAPSTONE PRESS
a capstone imprint

Pebble Plus is published by Capstone Press,
1710 Roe Crest Drive, North Mankato, Minnesota 56003
www.mycapstone.com

Library of Congress Cataloging-in-Publication Data
Names: Morey, Allan, author.
Title: Papillons / by Allan Morey.
Description: North Mankato, Minnesota : Capstone Press, [2017] | Series:
  Pebble plus. Tiny dogs | Audience: Ages 4-7. | Audience: K to grade 3. |
  Includes bibliographical references and index.
Identifiers: LCCN 2016006877| ISBN 9781515719656 (library binding) | ISBN
  9781515719717 (ebook (pdf)
Subjects: LCSH: Papillon dog—Juvenile literature.
Classification: LCC SF429.P2 M67 2017 | DDC 636.76—dc23
LC record available at https://lccn.loc.gov/2016006877

Editorial Credits
Emily Raij editor; Juliette Peters, designer;
Pam Mitsakos, media researcher; Laura Manthe, production specialist

Photo Credits
iStockphoto: Bigandt_Photography, 13; Shutterstock: DegtyaryovAndrey, 18–19, kostolom3000,
3, back cover top left, Mikkel Bigandt, 1, 20–21, Sergey Lavrentev, cover, 7, 15, Sheeva1, 9, vlastas,
design element throughout book, Zuzule, 5, 11; Thinkstock: Lenorlux, 17

Note to Parents and Teachers

The Tiny Dogs set supports national science standards related to life science. This book describes
and illustrates papillons. The images support early readers in understanding the text. The
repetition of words and phrases helps early readers learn new words. This book also introduces
early readers to subject-specific vocabulary words, which are defined in the Glossary section. Early
readers may need assistance to read some words and to use the Table of Contents, Glossary, Read
More, Internet Sites, Critical Thinking Using the Common Core, and Index sections of the book.

Printed in the United States of America.
009656F16

TABLE OF CONTENTS

BUTTERFLY EARS

Papillons are one of many tiny dogs. But they have something that makes them stand out. They have ears like butterfly wings. Papillon is the French word for butterfly.

In the 1500s people bred these tiny dogs from hunting dogs called spaniels. They now make great family dogs. They are good with kids and other pets.

SILKY AND SMART

Papillons are easy to carry around.

They are about as big as

a basketball. They weigh

6 to 9 pounds (2.7 to 4 kilograms).

Papillons have long, silky coats.
They have white fur with colored
markings. These spots can be black,
tan, brown, or red.

Papillons are smart.
These playful dogs are easy
to train. They like to do tricks
to please their owners.

PAPILLONS AS PETS

Papillons do not need a lot of room. They are great pets for people in apartments or small houses. But they may become nervous if left alone often.

Papillons need to be socialized as puppies. They should meet other dogs and people. If not, they might fear strange dogs and people.

Do you like to run and play catch? Papillons do. They have a lot of energy. They need to get lots of exercise. Healthy, active papillons live up to 16 years.

Papillons would rather play

than sit in your lap.

Race around your yard.

They will join in the fun!

GLOSSARY

breed—to mate and produce young

coat—an animal's hair or fur

exercise—a physical activity done in order to stay healthy and fit

hunting—to find and catch animals for food

marking—a patch of color on fur

nervous—upset or tense

socialize—to train to get along with people and other dogs

spaniel—a hunting dog with wavy fur and long ears

strange—not known or seen before

train—to prepare for something by learning or practicing new skills

READ MORE

Heos, Bridget. *Do You Really Want a Dog?* Do You Really Want? Mankato, Minn.: Amicus, 2014.

Markovics, Joyce. *Papillon: Monsieur Butterfly.* Little Dogs Rock! New York: Bearport Publishing, 2011.

Stainton, Sue. *I Love Dogs!* New York: Katherine Tegen Books, 2014.

INTERNET SITES

FactHound offers a safe, fun way to find Internet sites related to this book. All of the sites on FactHound have been researched by our staff.

Here's all you do:

Visit *www.facthound.com*

Type in this code: 9781515719656

Super-cool stuff!

Check out projects, games and lots more at
www.capstonekids.com

CRITICAL THINKING
USING THE COMMON CORE

1. Why do you think a papillon would be a good pet?
   (Integration of Knowledge and Ideas)

2. Why does a papillon need to be socialized?
   (Key Ideas and Details)

INDEX